The Tao of Twang

The Tao of Twang

Poems by Tim Hunt

CW Books

© 2014 by Tim Hunt

Published by CW Books
P.O. Box 541106
Cincinnati, OH 45254-1106

ISBN: 9781625490674
LCCN: 2013958468

Poetry Editor: Kevin Walzer
Business Editor: Lori Jareo

Visit us on the web at www.readcwbooks.com

Acknowledgments

Grateful acknowledgment is made to the editors of the magazines in which the following poems first appeared:

Cloudbank: "White Levis," "Why Redneck Western Poets Write the Way We Do," "The Daily Run," and "I Can Tell You Are a Logger"

Grasslimb: "Yes, Ma'am," "Still Life with Candy Machine and Boy," & "Pump Handle"

I.S.L.E.: "First Light (Desert Valley)" & "The Way Down"

Lummox: "Here and There"

Review Americana: "Rag Rug"

Rhino: "Preaching the Gospel" & "Still Life with Ash Tray and Beer Can"

Spoon River Poetry Review: "Remembering"

Storyscape: "Dr. Twang once had"

"Hearing Is Believing," "You Might Be," "Redneck Yoga," and "Memphis Tweet" first appeared in the chapbook *Redneck Yoga* (Finishing Line Press).

"Anecdote of the Jar" and "Depending: Three Side Yard Scenes on a Borrowed Image" first appeared in the chapbook *Thirteen Ways of Talking to a Blackbird* (Finishing Line Press).

for Susan, who finds the positive in the oddest things and has a most exceptional ear for Twang

Table of Contents

Foreword

Having won a major poetry prize Tim Hunt quit writing poetry for 20 years; instead he studied, taught and wrote as a scholar of American Literature (Jeffers, Kerouac).

> *Part of it (I came to realize as I puzzled over Robinson Jeffers, his practice and his critical dismissal) had to do with having been taught to think of the page as a surface on which one inscribed writing when what I wanted/needed to do was think of the page as a medium where enacted speech was stored for hearing.*

With *The Tao of Twang* we know in a new way this central issue with the reigning poetics, the competing gospels. Hunt engages our conundrum on the highly intellectual level of the scholar poet, opening the consideration of his poetry as a major statement, or at least a major question.

> *What if Wallace Stevens imagined talking to a blackbird rather than looking at one, or if William Carlos Williams had pulled back from that red wheelbarrow to include the side yard with the chickens within the frame, or if the "you" in "The Love Song of J. Alfred Prufrock" replied to "Let us go, then, you and I"?*

Well, we would be back to our families, our home towns

(in the rural ones, anyway), back to the ideologies, faiths, and aesthetics we came from but to which we now no longer (exactly) belong. The subject matter of these poems stems from a fidelity to "the living tradition" of his working/rural class/western background but his probing intellect on this subject uses the forms, constructs and aesthetics of academia, resulting in an ironic fidelity, root-deep. In his uses of the rich poetic clichés, the puns and profound mentality, mannerisms and aesthetics—the vanishing lingo of the rural west— the cultural caricatures become meaningful archetypes. *"In their poem/ the words mustn't be cut away." "In real stories/ what happens is never/ the point."* Writing from an "I" you aren't, can't be, can't come from or tell of, to a "you" you'll never know, a you who is not real, not there, just little scriggly black and white lines: both cultures, it becomes comically clear, are of faith, ideology, belief. *"And in this photo that does not// exist the preacher is beyond the frame."* Yes, that is the gospel truth, the twang of the Tao, but for Heaven's sake, who is the preacher? (Could the enforced taboo of the "I" be the disguised "I" of the ruling class?) Indirectly, delightfully, his poems put the Holy Writ of academia's canon under the same lens as it puts the culture of his roots.

> *In all its uses, the Tao is considered to have ineffable qualities that prevent it from being defined or expressed in words. However, the Tao can be known or experienced, and its principles, which can be discerned by observing Nature, can be followed or practiced or in some*

way entered into relationship with. (Wikipedia)

Hilarious, thought-provoking, deeply philosophical, sometimes almost transhuman, to use Jeffers word, in the mix of subject and form from two different/almost at-war cultures, and with the help of his fantastic ear, you will know the Tao of twang. You will know why redneck Western poets write the way we do. And you will newly ponder, again, our aesthetic assumptions.

Sharon Doubiago
August, 2013

SECTION ONE

Another Way

Remove the words, each
One until the few
    d • o • t
The white sand—
A rock garden.

Perhaps a gingko.
Whether the green
Is there
Or the eye sees
As if it is
Does not matter.

Make the poem
Of what isn't there.

        *

Or sit where the river
Cuts beneath the rock,
The light stepping
Across the water. But do not
Watch the light, watch
The water, until the day
Is the one moment

When the current
Disappears and you see
Into the river.

         *

But in this celebration
the three women drinking iced
tea, Lipton's, are sisters, telling
stories that start somewhere and never
quite end, because in real stories
what happens is never
the point. Turn and turn
about, they stack the mismatched
bits higher, higher, then build
again, as if these moments and
remembered somethings are blocks, each
side with a painted letter, an image, a
moment. In their poem
the words mustn't be cut away. In
their poem the words must
tumble, then pool out as the creek
does, pausing to gather again.
Close your eyes.
Listen.

Hearing Is Believing

Do not, I say, trust your eye.
It tells you, true, which
Of "two," "to," "2," and "too"
Are the same and not,

But if you believe your eye,
Twang is only the *thing* and not
The *thang*. So trust your ears,
For they know the difference

'Tween Thing and Thang
Is as much as everything.

Instructions for Remembering the Grange Hall, Middletown, California

Imagine it is late afternoon, perhaps mid-
August. Town's back that way. You can
walk it—a few miles, thistle and red dirt.
But someone will drive the old man and his fiddle,

and his granddaughter will wear her cowgirl get up,
the one makes you swear she's Patsy Montana,
The Cowboy's Sweetheart, and she'll bring
her guitar. She's a pretty sight and can play, too.

And the old man can still make you want
to dance, even after the week working in the sun,
even though the hall is nothing but a tin roof
on pine boards and there seems no end

to the hay to buck, fence to mend, stock
to water, or the clothes in the zinc lined tub,
chickens to feed, the birthing, dying, bread to knead,
the empty distance to the hills if one looks up.

Tonight you will wash up and comb a little shoe dye
through your hair. Tonight you will walk to the
    Grange Hall.

Anecdote of the Jar

Up on a hill in Tennessee
I took a jar
And offered a salute.

The stars winked
As if in cahoots.
The white

Lightning jagged
Behind my eyes,
And I smashed that jar

Upon a rock,
Singing with the spirit
As if free of all

Dominion and
Welcomed by every
Weed and brush

Thicket. And jigging
To the whine of the barn
Dance fiddle in my ears,

I left those shards
Where they fell about
That rock and walked

Down through the trees
That grew across that hill,
Back down to this

Human thing, the heart.

Still Life with Ash Tray and Beer Can

See how carefully the cigarette's gray bloom
Poses, a dancer
Standing on the ball of one foot—
Arm and hand,
Her fingers completing the arc.

The crumpled can, too, leans as if pulling
Against a tether; the punched
Triangles in the top,
Black against the silvered metal.

We must imagine, it seems,
The calendar and window,
The vague wall's routine
Paraphernalia…and the hand
That will reach into the puddled light,
It too is a shadow.

Class Party

Here's something you can mock—
A singer with a big hat
Singing through his nose, the electric
Fiddle squiggling the pitch
Like a palsied icer decorating
A Sam's Club sheet cake. You see, today
Even country folk are allowed to think

They have a place in the rodeo
And pretend they are consumer cowboys
Riding the electric bull up and down
The wide aisles, so long
As the paycheck lasts and the credit
Holds, so long as they are

Punched in and out down at the factory—
Folded, spindled, and neatly
Sent for another weekend ride
Of being free. And it is true
Some will drape a see-through
Stars & Bars in the pickup's
Rear window through which you

Cringe at the hunting rifle

And what you take to be merely naïve
Hate, but alas that flag is not just
A love for some simplistic past
That was a lie but instead, or maybe
Only as well, a way of resisting
You because they know that *something*

Is a lie and *somewhere* there is
A joke in all this, and they know
They should not be laughing.

Redneck Yoga

You might be a redneck
If your idea of Yoga
Is Downward Facing Log

And you have practiced
This pose in the weeds
Of the front yard

Beside that piece of shit
Chevy up on blocks
Needing a new clutch—

The handful of bolts
Rusting in the hubcap
That collects the morning

Dew and glints the noon
Against the torn shade
Of the doublewide's

Kitchen window.

"One Piece at a Time" aka Heads or Tails

In that song where Johnny celebrates
sneaking out his Psychobilly Cadillac
one piece at a time—nestling the link
rods in the lunch box, potato chip
salt flecking the carburetor's sheen,
and another day of fitting the same
fucking front right hub cap on the same
fucking front right wheel over and over—
you can hear the pride of chumping the boss
like it's Friday night and you can
punch any combination you
want on the juke box as you
lift another just when you please.

And then there's Tennessee Ernie Ford
singing "16 Tons," tunneling down
from Merle's folksy take into that darker seam
where getting nothing is truly getting
nothing as you spend the company store
scrip until you're spent and from up
the holler you hear a front porch fiddle—
a double stopped perfect fifth, then a note
drawing down as if it marked an end to your shift.

Depending: Three Side Yard Scenes on a Borrowed Image

1.

the rusted
barrow

darkened
red from

the rain, the
feathers slick

in her hand,
the bright

pulse spattering
the weeds.

2. (Still Life with Cook Stove and Window)

so much depends
on the sun
glinting the skin
of rainwater,
the wheel

barrow tipped
so you can't see
its muddied cave
as you glance
from the window—
another reminder
of the things you
mustn't mention
as you finger
the bruises above
your wrist—the
ones that are
fading beneath
the thinning cotton.

3. (This is just to say...)

yes, I
see

the angled
light

as if the
clouds

are torn

curtains

and how
the storm's

sheen is
a kind of music—

the wheel
barrow a red

calliope,
but if you

want more
than biscuits,

get me
a chicken, that

white
one by

the fence.

Folk Song

Froggy went a-courtin' and he did
Ride, but the song doesn't tell
What he rode, just that he had sword
And pistol by his side. Maybe Froggy
Rode a Tennessee stud—a gentleman
Frog, maybe he was Colonel Froggy.
But where I heard that song, Froggy
Musta rode a cow pony or maybe a freight
Wagon mule, green feet flapping
As if he were W.C. Fields, both hands
Hanging to the pommel and wishing
He could let loose and grab for that
Pint of rye.

           Thinking back, how
He and Miss Mousey were to,
As one might say, hop along
After he asked her to be his bride,
I don't know. And when the old man
Would sing that song, the fiddle laid along
His forearm, almost in his lap, all he had
In his eye was a twinkle, and the boy
Who listened hadn't read none of that Freud
But knew courting must be

Serious business if Froggy was
That into his equipment.

Rag Rug

The lamp's brass plating
gleams in the light that reaches to her hands
twisting the bits of cloth into a cord
the thickness of her index finger
to coil into a rag rug. In the hills
where she is from even rags are not to waste.
I would ask her if I could
whether it matters that the cotton strip
is from the girl's special dress
or that the flannel, torn across
the angle of the squares,
is from her father's shirt, the one
he liked to wear Friday nights
as they walked into town
and the light cleaned up after
its busy day and the crickets
chattered as if sitting on the porch
having a smoke. What she liked
best was the walk home after
the barn dance, the air a nice warm,
the dirt soft on bare feet and the fire flies
as if the stars had come down to visit
and one brought a fiddle.

But rags are, I think, only things
not to waste, the way lard
can be made soap or a frock cut down
and worn again, or shoes stuffed with paper
and made to fit. And this rocking, the
twisting of torn cloth between thumb and fingers
is not remembering, nor quite
forgetting either.

Preaching the Gospel

In this photo that does not exist,
The girl is perhaps four, the frock
Full over thin legs, a bow in her hair

As the heat fills the small town
Mississippi church and she
Frowns upon the folding chair

Collapsed, as if from the heat,
And even through the silence echoing
That clatter and thump, the grayed

Chemicals shading the paper, it is clear
She is preaching upon that chair
For its sins damning it to hell

In the name of the lord stupid
Sonabitchin-geesus-chrise chair.
And in this photo that does not

Exist the preacher is beyond the frame,
And her aura is luminous
As the congregation turns to her sermon

And her father's eyes
Offer up an Amen to her
Righteousness.

You Might Be

1.

You might be a redneck
If you know that poor
Is poor and it pisses you off

That people in town think
That's what you are
And sometimes you want to piss

Them off because you know
That poor is not what you are
Though you are.

You might be a redneck
If you sometimes think
Redneck is a color

And you know you're
Not supposed to say *that*
Or *think* it, and that too

Pisses you off.

You might be a redneck
If your family tree
Is a map of snarled routes—

West Virginia, Missouri,
The California Ozarks
But always the hill country.

You might not be a redneck
If you think to call this
Scots-Irish Diaspora, but know

Yer not 'sposed to say or think
That either, then sure as shit
Ya probably are.

2.

You might be a redneck if
You think diphthong is somthin'
Dirty as in "Diphthong, me baby

In the Tunnel of Love," or as in
That country song someone must
Have written but the radio won't play:

"My diphthong's too big fer this

Trowjan" and in your mind's ear
Ya hear this done Bakersfield Sound

With the treble on the Fender
Cranked all the way up to
Chalk-on-Blackboard and to barbwire

Cutting your sorry ass as you
Beat it out the back door and over
The fence as Missy's legal number one

Guy, who really is your cousin, but
Not hers, tries to draw a bead on what
Sure would be a sorry ass if he weren't

Too drunk to aim and if, as Missy
Likes to say, "Ah, that little gun,
All it shoots are blanks."

3.

And then you could be
A redneck if you remember
That trailer out behind

Your grandparents' house,
Maybe twelve feet long and six wide,

41

Tar paper roof and the sides

Of wood, two small windows
On each side—that one place
In all the shouting and hurt

Stares when you were still
Too young to know what
These things meant, where the light

Seemed something to touch
With your open hand as it sieved
Through the screen door

And you listened again
To the old woman tell the stories
You no longer remember

Though you really wish you
Could and so pretend you do
And that too pisses you off.

SECTION

TWO

Memphis Tweet aka Blue Moon of Tweet 'Cause It Ain't Alright Mama

In the Kingdom of the Blind
The one-eyed Tweet is King
And the one-eyed Jack

Swivels his hips. He has not
Left the building. His paunch
And marbled fat of his butt

Bulge the white leather as if
Sausage stuffed in a sheep
Gut casing, and he has, Oh

The shame, nearly forgotten
The sagging bed springs, the
Reverbed twang of Heartbreak Hotel

Emptier than the sky, black
Beyond the neon.

'Til Twangdom Come

Although some worship
In the Church of Fender
And solemnly read

The Book of Telecaster,
There are many rooms
In God's holy mansion,

Each soaked in reverb.
And while the Logos is
Always one, it is a chord—

The root and perfect fifth
Absolute no matter how
The third wanders in search

Of Twangdom Come.

The Tao of Twang

The sound
Of one hand clapping—
Ripples
In a still pond,
The pebble
Of silence.

The sound
Of one string twanging—
A spinning
Knife
Biting
The dead oak.

*

In the Kingdom of
Twang, there is
No past, only
Present, for in
That Kingdom
Ring and Rang
Are truly one.

In the Kingdom of

Twang, there is
No future, only
Present,
For in that Kingdom
What might come
Is already done.

*

In the east
Yin and Yang
Enfold, no
Beginning
Or end, light
Unto dark
Balanced back
Again.

In
This world
Of tequila sunrise
And sunset
One is one
Instead of two
Is one: Twin
Twang which is
To say Twang

And Twang—
An E string struck
Twice, the vacuum
Tube glowing
Against the bar's
Darkened wall
As one and one
Look to be
One, which is
Two and not
Transcendent even
If they complete
First the rhyme
Of two and then
The rhyme of one.

      *

The Tao of Twang
Is not one way
But many: there
Is trout stream, the mind
Become water,
One with
Smoothed rock.
And the zen
Of panning, a slow

Rocking, the eye
Knowing the gravel
For what it is, then
The bit of nugget
Says here I am. Too,
There is the waiting
Of deer blind, the
Horizons within
The gnarled
Manzanita thickets.
And the art of sitting,
Elbow on bar as if
The tapered pipe of glass
In the hand mattered,
Watching without
Watching as one might
Watch the surface
Of the water or the path
Beyond the blind
Knowing that hoping
Will make it not so,
Knowing one must
Become one
With the waiting.

*

The Tao of Twang
Is like a walnut:
The tan shell
Smooth to the finger,
The meat rich
On the tongue.

Sometimes I think
The shell is irreverence,
Reverence the nut
Meat. Sometimes
I think it is
The other way around.

But that is wrong.
If there is only reverence
And irreverence, then where
Is the nothing
From which they spring
And to which
They belong?

Dr. Twang once had

a real name—Bobby Bob
Smith or Emmanuel Heath Edwards
Clinton or some such,

But even he was hard-pressed
To remember it. He was
Twang, or simply Doc. Think of him

In profile, black Stetson
Slicing a pale moon, a street
Lamp trailing the frame's edge

As he strides the empty sidewalk
After the gig toward some dingy room
Guitar case in hand—years and years of road,

His name fading like ink on a paper
Scrap weathering in the cycle of rain
And sun, until one with the ditch,

And even the paper faded away.
Twang could still summon
That other name, but it no longer mattered.

He was the Twang he'd become—the
Smoky nights of darkened dancers
Milling the bar floors. Twang was,

He knew, only an excuse as they
Lonelied with laughing or smugly
Appraising or needing eyes,

And his fingers walked yet again
The guitar's neck of touch-worn
Rosewood. Twang knew all the tricks—

How to pick right at the bridge to get
That cue ball click, how to run the table
Like Lester Flatt's G-run on a Martin

D-28, and the slow bends up the neck
So the strings sound like slow dance denim
On the jeans she shouldn't wear. He knew

The pulls and slurs, the hammer-ons
That made each walk never the same
As he tossed lick after lick

Into the spilled beer smell and cigarette
Haze—the Friday night cologne

Like foam laced atop a wave.

He knew they never really listened, or rather
They listened through him, hearing
Their needs and wants. Twang remembered

Driving a back road off the two-lane
Between Reno and Vegas. To the East,
A slash of rain along a far ridge, the cloud

A torn pillow trailing its stuffing,
The smell sharp as an old mattress
Rank with pee against the dry of the desert.

He didn't remember why he'd turned
West at the whorehouse, the idling semis
Like spokes from the manufactured

Homes circled like wagon train wagons
In a western movie. But two valleys
Into the mountains he passed an old Airstream

Set up from the road where a dirt track
Wound back, perhaps to one of those mines
That had paid big back when Tonopah

Was a place to be instead of pass through.
Even from the road Twang could see
The dents on the Airstream's body

And sense the oxidized pitting that dulled
The aluminum skin as if it were a beer can
Tossed into the ditch, and Twang saw

The windows—open, the white curtains.
Cheap, Penny's or K-Mart, where they'd looked
Lacy through the plastic, now dulled

In the sun but still trying to be something
Nice. After that it no longer mattered
That he was an occasion. Each night

He wrapped himself in their cigarette smoke
And gave what he could. His fingers
No longer walked the paths he'd learned

But followed where they led, playing
For the girl who'd put up the curtains
And the shadowed space within the pitted trailer

And for the relief from the shadowed space
Which was the darkened neon

Of their dancing. Each night he played

As if their needs were blessings
They offered, and he played
For the sky beyond the evening's

Smoky room and the empty space beyond
The trailer, and when he could
He played, too, for the wind—

The ever-patient ostinato to the coyotes'
Laugh in those hours after the bars
Have closed.

T. Texas Twiddle Reflects Upon His First Roundup

The corral, a tent of dust—the hooves
Of the young steers scrabbling for footing
As the cowboys held them down and the iron
Szzzed through the hair, charring
The flank's blank page. Leaning

The rail, T. Texas could see the brown
Eyes roll, their tongues loll, the ropy spit,
As the rancher's wife slipped her knife
Again, so deftly through the sack's slack
Skin—a glint of light, then dark blood

As she tossed the oysters into a pan, promising
The cowboys she'd share if they held on tight.
T. Texas wasn't old enough to understand
That look in her eyes, but already he knew
You wouldn't want to be the rancher.

T. Texas Ponders the Scene

T. Texas was drinking his Café Americano
Back to the wall and watching the window
Like a true cowboy should and watchin', too,
The young'uns with their grandé skinny
Whatsits lattés and god knows what
Sprinkled on top. *Geeyahd.* What had the world
Come to? T. warmed his hands, cupping
His cup, remembering when Java and Joe
And Swill were all the same thing as you leaned
To the counter and an aproned cutie
Curtseyed a fresh pot toward your mug.

T. Texas surveyed the scene: the java jockeys
Who knew they were cool, the kid staring
At the table top like it was his navel and he
Might fall in, and Miss Spike with the dog
Collar and tattoo shawl tonguing her foam
Like a kitten testing a saucer of milk. These
He sorta understood. It was the foursome
In the middle he wondered at—their heads
Bobbing as if to each other, fingers mumbling
Like nuns txting their beads, praying to be heard.

In Which T. Texas Twiddle Goes All Troubador

When it come to music, T. Texas was deep
Into Ernest Tubb, "Waltzing Across Texas"
And "I Hate to See You Go." Now, true,
He could make room for Bob Wills and "Panhandle
Rag." And "San Antonio Rose" and "Roly
Poly" were the real stuff, but Bob was a dance
Hall kinda guy all kick up your heels and Yee Ha
Hip flask and sweaty smile. It was Ernest
Who knew the pine planks of "Walking the Floor
Over You" and the wind doing steel guitar
Through the barn loft, the empty fields
Waiting for dawn as if *that* would mean
Something. Ah, Billy Byrd, pick one. Pick it pretty.

T. Texas at the Red Light

T. Texas knew that real men
Rode horses but he wasn't
Into ass thumping whether
Saddled or bare back. Far
As he was concerned a real ride
Had a rear view mirror, and so
Much hood it mighta been a prairie
As he idled at the light, left
Arm resting on the open window
Sucking on a hand rolled as the
World walked by. T. Texas
Knew he wasn't the show
But then again he knew how
To watch it.

Why T. Texas Wasn't NRA

Now, T. Texas did admire John Wayne—that
Stand your ground slow to anger high
Noon of draw only when you must, shoot
Once, and walk away. And Roy Rogers, too,
Cause he could sing a pretty lead to the Sons
Of the Pioneers doing fourths and fifths in harmony
Yet still draw quick if rustler Russ wouldn't
Blend his voice around the campfire. So, yes,
T. Texas was a Second Amendment kinda guy.
Out on the trail, ya needed a Colt on your hip
Or better a Winchester for that rattlesnake
That might spook the herd; or that stray deer
Fan dancing some mesquite, flashing a little
Thigh, calling Hey, Big Guy, Wouldn't I
Roast up nice for dinner tonight? But T. Texas
Wasn't that down with Dirty Harry
Or Rambo either. Too many bullets spoiled
The meat, and he liked to hear the boys
Singing home Home on the Range dipping
Their sourdough in a little redeye gravy,
And between songs you could hear the stars
Like they was violins on the soundtrack.

T. Texas Runs an Errand

T. Texas was in need
Of a calendar and so he
Moseyed down to Otto's Auto
Parts for this year's twelve
Part harmony of Miss Honey
And Miss Heather and all
Their demure friends. He
Was a connoisseur of all
The ways a young lady
Could caress a shock absorber
So carefully angled into
The scene. And too the gleam
Of her chassis as if chamois-
Shined by the light and lens.
Ah, T. Texas could
Almost agree that what
Mattered was pure form, the
Platonic ideal more real than
The real, but much as he loved
The contemplative life
And took scholarly pleasure
In the multiple possibilities of spark
Plugs and pistons—the infinite
Array of positions—he was,

In fact, more truly committed

To the materialism

Of dialectical interplay.

T. Texas Joins The Party

Where T. Texas lived wacky weed
Was still illegal, even if your bunions ached,
So thought maybe he'd join the Tea
Party and bought him some rolling
Papers, zipped his Zippo and went
Off to the rally, all ready to be a true
In—dee—vis—ible Indyvidyouall
And declare his Liberty
And Death opposition to guvmint
Hand outs and hand jobs. He was
For damn sure tired a being jerked
Around and ready to stand
His ground and knew someone
There would tell him just where
That ground could be found
And whether to flick his Bic and wave
It over his head or wave his middle
Finger instead, and either way
Was sure he'd know he was
One with the Founding
Fathers who fer damn sure
Didn't believe in Guvmint 'cause
Every Revolution is every man

With a gun telling The Man
What to stick and where to stick it.

T. Texas, Contemplating His Brethren Portraying His Brethren, Avers That Indeed There Is a Difference Between Corn Pone and Corn Ball

Though Jeff Foxworthy (who knows better but
pretends he don't) can tell the difference 'tween "ya'all"
and a yachter's "yawl," and that a Tuxedo ain't
a napkin under your chin (as in "tucks les eat, oh")
and that a daisy chain in a double wide ain't
a redneck rondo, there's money in Bubba-dom,
as in Bubba-dumb, and true some Bubbas are
pretty damn dumb, but there is a difference,
as T. Texas knew, 'tween corn pone and corn
ball. One you et cause you were poor
and hadta. The other? Oh, it's all Cracker
Jack and always at the bottom a two bit piece
a shit plastic toy stuck to that sugar-coated
peanut just to make you feel like Fate
done flashed ya a beaver shot, then flipped
you off as she walked away, your hand full
a that empty foil package.

In which T. Texas Twiddle Is Not Thinking of The Snow Man or the Coke Dealer on the Corner or How He'd Been Snow Jobbed at Wally's Wonder World of Used Cars (aka To Signify or Not to Signify, That Is the Question)

T. Texas had heard that Cousin Jimmy Joe's
nephew Billy Bob, who lots of folks
called the Bobber for no good reason he
could think of, was telling folks there was
a differ'nce 'tween something called
a signifier and the signified and that this
meant that words didn't mean nothin'. Now
you could, he thought, see this as a reason
not to let the young ones go off to school,
but being young was a time to fool
around, then ya had to marry and settle
down. Too much gun play and someone's
daddy'd take that shotgun off the wall (Shoulda,
Boy, kept the safety on or better left it
in the holster)—all this in a manner of
speaking, of course. Anyway, T.
Texas sure as shit knew that words
meant something. When you stepped in it

and muttered Shit that's Shit, what could
be plainer than that—as folks did say
It happens, and iffen it don't, goose
grease was a sure-fire load lightener. Such
silly words. T. Texas, spite of himself,
found he was wondering if he was a
signified or a signifier. Or maybe he was
just signifying. He'd heard LeRoy down
at the feedstore say "Don't you be signifyin'."
Maybe LeRoy'd set him straight. He sure as
Shit wasn't going to ask the Bobber, who all
ready, he was pretty sure, thought he didn't
know nuthin and didn't know that nuthin's
already a lot to know.

T. Texas Considers a Career in Politics

T. Texas was sitting on the park bench,
the one in the shade where the path
sunned by, his crossed legs stretched

so the lizard skin toes of his boots each
angled toward a pine tree and his Stetson
down as if he and it were taking a nap.

T. Texas liked to watch the young ladies
stroll, their shiny running shorts,
the infinite rhythms that were

in a sense only walking. What puzzled
him though was PINK written
over and over as if they were each

a candy bar racked next to the checkout
line. Why not Snickers or Mars Bars,
Even Payday. He didn't think U-No and Baffle

Bars still existed but T. Texas believed
in variety and truth in advertising. He did
of course know about branding—that uniform

stamp that made the cows a herd, and this
was maybe why he wondered at PINK—
embossed over and over as if they were

a herd. T. Texas studied how they each
filled their wrappings, the distinctive
motions within the one, and then he knew

his calling—to bust 'em out from that corral,
to free them from PINK, and he began to write
their poem as they each walked by:

Instead of PINK, she would be *You Wish*
and she *Mount Doom* and she *Cheek
to Cheek* and she *Hole in One*

and she would simply have a hand
print on each cheek and she *Third eye
Blind* and she *Mine* and and and…

Each would freely choose from his designer
catalogue, the website he'd create, the late
night infomercials for the ones

watching Doris Day movies
pacing themselves through a box
of sampler chocolates. T.

Texas smiled beneath the brim
of his Stetson. He would help them be
all they could be, and they would truly be

free.

T. Texas Twiddle Remembers Learning the Facts of Life

This was 1939, maybe 1940, thereabouts,
and T. Texas just a boy
riding his first round up with the men
who sat so easy in the saddle
their cigarettes seemed to roll themselves
when they'd duck the brim of their
work Stetsons, then look back up
and take that first draw, the left hand
lazy at their sides, the right holding
the reins up for show as a real fancy
lady'd hold one of them bone china teacups
standing to be admired in Miss Maudie
May's parlor. T. Texas hadn't
ever been in Maudie May's but he'd heard
talk and seen pictures and thought
it must be like that.

T. Texas watched everything trying to know
what to do next. Especially he watched
the men. It seemed their eyes were always
on the horizon, steady
on the emptiness beyond the range of hills,
their knees moving the ponies as they

drove the herd out from the gap
and across the valley. T. Texas wondered
what they saw in that empty sky
beyond the hills and how many years
it took to see it, but there was, he knew,
no way to ask or for them to tell it.

Later at the ranch the cowboy with the white
moustache sat on the pickup's running board,
leaning onto his knees as he tapped
a line of Prince Albert the length of the paper.
T. Texas watched closely, imagining his fingers
would someday be so knowing, and neither
of them paid the old cow any mind
as she drifted up, lifted her tail, the brown
stream spattering the door and down
the side of the cowboy's face. He licked
the edge, rolled it, flicked the match. T. Texas
waited as if he weren't shuffling his feet.
"Ain't ya gonna Wipe it off?" "Nah,"
the cowboy said, "Comes off better dry." T.
Texas looked down at the toe of his boot,
then up at the horizon, and waited.

SECTION
THREE

First Light (Desert Valley)

Where sometimes there's water—
A spring squall that somehow topped
The mountain wall or a late snow
Gathering a dry channel—wild
Flowers bloom a moment as the mesquite
Readies for another arc of summer—
Bits of life edging out from the rocks,
The light behind the ridge
Pecking the dark's thinned shell.

"I Can Tell You Are a Logger"

In the song, the waitress knows you are a logger
'cause you stir your coffee with your thumb,
and she sings you verse after verse of her lost
logger love who walked out into the wind
of some past winter, his mackinaw left
on the bunkhouse peg, and finally froze to death
at a gazillion degrees below.
He too stirred his coffee with his thumb like all true
logger men do. But you are not a logger man, you
are a boy sitting cross-legged near the heat stove,
your cup of chocolate warm in your hands
and the woman who sings to you is not a waitress,
but a logger woman married to a logger man,
and she knows how silly the verses are and just
how silly they are not, and perhaps she senses
how the song is like a ridge top—a looking back
to what was and down the slope of what will
no longer be when true logger men will no
longer be, and no one will stir
their coffee with their thumb.

A Triptych for Oliver Hillman
(Satley, California)

1. (Still Life at Dawn with Trailer and Wrench)

The bark of old growth Doug fir
Has a reddish hue, but this
Is a charcoal drawing
So that the canopy's dark green
Doesn't quite erase the trailer
Framed in the bit of clearing.

Already the truck is gone.
In this scale the tripod and
Engine hoist, the boxes of tools
Are gray smudges as if rocks
Or bits of scrub. But notice

To the right, off center,
The wrench for the hub of a D8
Cat, leaned against a tree,
The jaw a sixteen inch span, the smoothed
Oak handle taller than a man.

It too is out of scale, but notice
In the first light

Nothing is out of place

2. (Eating Poetry)

There is almost light
On the rock flank. Soon
Enough the morning
Will burn through the timber.
But for the moment, as
The black thins, I am eating
Poetry—a short stack,
One egg sunnyside, a thick
Slice of ham, bone in
With the dab of marrow.
And after, the bitter
Coffee, brewed by the woman
With the tired face,
Who watches the counter as we eat.
Soon, it will be time to go—
To pick up the load.
But for now there is
Almost light along the ridge
As she fills my cup
And takes the empty plate.

3. (The Daily Run)

The weight of the load
Is a kind of pleasure—
The logs wanting to drive
The trailer straight
Down the mountain,
The synchronizing of clutch
And brakes, double shifting,
The cab deflecting them
Turn by turn until the snaked
Dirt of the temporary road
Turns onto the pavement
And one can ease back
Against the seat, light
A cigarette and think about
Whatever the day has also
Put before you. Better
Is the empty run, the diesel
Singing its ease even
On the grade, the sawdust burner
Glowing in the mirror,
Growing smaller, then winking
Out as the road turns and it is dusk.

In the Mountains

In the mountains it is still as if
not now. Or seems that way
as you reach into the pick up bed for the chain saw, the
high air still morning cold as you walk to the fire
scorched fir marked for harvest. In the days
before not now you know that two men would have
cut this tree, joined by the long saw, a serrated strap,
back and forth, through the ringed layers, but that was
then, and this is not now and your eyes follow up
the ridge, your hand yanking the cord, the saw
firing up, waiting for you to squeeze the trigger.

In the mountains you do not think about lumber.
You think about logs, chaining them up, settling
them into the trailer's arms, the skid road
to the mill, the road back to the circle
of trees where you live and the light is never
still because the needles of the high branches
are never still. Sometimes at night your wife still
takes the guitar from behind the chair. Sometimes
she sings "Red River Valley"; sometimes
"I Can Tell You're a Logger 'Cause You
Stir Your Coffee with Your Thumb."

In the mountains there are things you want—the
T-Bird coupe the bank took back that season
you were hurt and couldn't work, and your rig
is old—not baling wire and chewing gum, true,
but near enough. And it's not that you don't want
now. You just don't see the point of Ed
Sullivan and foofy dogs turning flips or Milton
Berle, the falling down as if that were
funny—those rooftop wires hooking you to now, to
Alka Seltzer, to Wonder Bread, to See
the USA in Your Chevrolet.

In the mountains you do not think about See the
USA or the foofy dogs. Sometimes you think
about sky, sometimes you worry about fire,
sometimes the bank that owns your rig as if
it owned you and could take you back like it
took the T-Bird. But there aren't wires yet
in the trees hooking you to somewhere and you
can, for the moment, work as if alone, thinking
trees, thinking logs, thinking not lumber, not
houses in rows tasseled with spiked wire
as if waiting to be harvested. In the mountains
it is still as if not now as you work to believe
in here and not the there that is now.

Remembering

To be the listener, the watcher
Is an office, not in the political sense,
But still a kind of election.

Perhaps it is the chance of one's history.
Perhaps something already
In the way the nerves are raveled

And the body's specific palette
Of chemicals. It is not a choice
Exactly, but still it can be refused.

                    *

Sometimes what we hear
Is the past as if we are
Watching: those scars

Within the brain that become
A mind—points where the weave
Of the nerves carries shadings

Or where it breaks, and the faint
Arc must somehow ford a gray
Looping creek to find a pathway

In the thicket on the other
Side. It can be hard to find
The way, hard to follow

The faint arc as it darts
Or pauses as if hiding in the hollowed
Trunk of a snag, where lightning

Once burned out the tree—as if
The arc felt a kinship
With that fire. But the kinship

You feel is with the hollowing,
As the flame seeps down
Into the space within the tree

Burning, even over years, until the tree
Is a thin tube, and a shear of wind
Snaps it clean, and now the seeping rain

Soaks the fibrous bark, slicks
The charred inner skin that is quilted
Like the lining of a coat.

*

To be the watcher, the listener
Is to follow the arc as it maps
And remaps the gray pathways that are

Never the same twice. The hollowed
Snags never in quite the same
Place. But they are there.

They are there, and it is your
Office to have listened, watched,
And so you walk the gray pathways

Of the gray thickets, finding again
The burned out snags, where they are
This time, and you pause

Fingering the lining of the coat,
Then hold your blackened fingers
Before you as if you held a lantern,

As if this would show you the way.
And perhaps it does as you wade across
A shallow stretch of creek

Looking for the path on the other side.

Pump Handle

In this photo that does not exist
The boy holds the pump handle as if it is
Taking him for a walk and he isn't sure
Where they are going. The pail, open
Mouthed, waits beneath the spout.

There is a secret to drawing water, one
The boy will grow up not needing to know.
And there is a secret that has drawn those
Who pause from the fried chicken and
The iced cream churned from the peaches
Behind the farm house and watch him
Thrust, yank the arm. This, too, no longer
The secret he will need to know.

Here and There

Place can be anywhere,
But is always
Somewhere and never
Simply what is
There. It has something
To do with how it was
At some odd moment.

This is why place is never public,
Never shared, though it seems
It should be. This is why
Place is always imagined when
We are somewhere else, in
Time, in terrain, among
Different people and things.

Place happens
When we are still
Able to imagine that the
World we are learning is
And will wait for us.

Perhaps place can happen
Again when we have

Come to know
This isn't so.

Place is not real, though
Of course it is.
Let me draw you a map.

Here, this dot was once
Place.

Doubled Exposure

1. (Bible Camp)

The man's voice is a room, you
can come in from the hallway
through the door. "Come," he says.
"Lay down your sins. Repent."
You listen. The trees have their backs
to you. Wrapped in their green coats
but standing tall, they are watching
the night. You watch
the other children hunched
on the folding chairs, the lights
on the fence posts stare down. No
one moves. They are one with
Him, their hair catching the light,
holding it. You look off, through
the fence at the trees just beyond
the light's shadow. "Repent.
Come." You do not know what
"Repent" means or "sin" but you
know "wrong," you know standing
in the hallway's shadow. "Come," he
says again, and you do, into that
temporary light, putting on

the voice, a coat with pockets. Others
come too. Together, you are warm
in the voice, together
you make a room for the voice.

2. (Camping by the Lake)

Late spring, no moon, the dark
beyond the fire and hill's black
shoulder so clear the stars are
so far they are forever. You hold
your hands up, the quick tongues
of heat licking your palms,
the arthritic Manzanita sticks
black within the flame.
The man and woman who are
your parents are each alone
in their own seam of heat and cold
looking past you at the water or
inward, you cannot tell. They, too,
are empty like the night, that hole
in the sky that shows you the space
between each bit of air, the separate
molecules, a stillness beyond
the brief flares the fire tosses
against the black—the sparks
for a moment stars, then not.

Belonging

When you walk away
you become
not of that place.

When you become
not of that place
you still belong

but in this different
belonging you are
outside the time

of those
to whom you belong.
In the world where

you do not belong
no one belongs.
That is why

you must remember
those to whom you belong
though you are

no longer within their time
even as they let you
come back as if you mattered

in that place, in
their time, in that belonging
that is not belonging.

Still Life with Victrola and Gravestone

In this photo that does not exist
The sun looks back through the screens
On the room once a porch. It pretends

To look in at the boy, but really what it cares about
Are the leaves of the black walnut tree
And the star thistle, the thorns rayed as if, too,

A kind of sun. How little it matters
That the boy has chosen a brittle disc,
Scratched with music. He offers it

To the Victrola, winds the crank,
And listens. He does not know who
Sings as if to him. He doesn't think

To imagine a time or place for the voice
Within the current of static, something
Graceful and pure, the needle's special noise

As it clatters round and round.
Nor does he understand the name or dates
Chiseled into the smoothed gray stone

He has climbed on to watch the arm
Ride the needle inward. After, in the
Silence, he will trace the stone's figures,

As if his finger might voice them, and later
Wonder how death becomes something
We climb on, then walk away

Slowly edging in as if there is music
Within the static as we remember
And forget until grief becomes

At last something we might stand on.

Still Life with Candy Machine and Boy

In this photo that does not exist
The boy is on a bench, sitting, the nurse
In the white shoes, turned slightly,

Looking over her left shoulder. He is
Maybe ten, chubby, the jeans rolled up—
Sitting very still, as if seeing nothing.

He has, it seems, emptied his face
Into a mask while he hides in the shadow
Behind the candy machine where the dark

Will be there even in the morning.

"Yes, Ma'am"

Working class—some of us are, you
know, each with a particular shame
we didn't realize was shame, the marking
we don't quite see but somehow know
the doctor's daughter and son of the man
who owns the hardware store know is there
even though they don't quite see the marking
either. Or maybe it's that they have secret
signs they share when you're not looking
so the teachers know they belong, and you
watch them closely as if you could steal
the signs and you, too, would belong. Or maybe
it's a kind of smell—the blood on your father's
shoes when he comes home at night and leaves
them outside on the porch, a smell that says sawdust
and hamburger twisting from the grinder's mouth
and the lady who must be served with that precise
roast cut only for her as you watch from the doorway—
the knife's stroke, the quick of the neatly
wrapping, the smile passed across the
silvery counter top and you still thinking
this is a special place—the sawdust with
its smell, the crate of iced chickens tucked
inside the cooler's door, the white apron,

the paper hat, the "Yes, Ma'am" as the chin
ducks so slightly you don't quite see it.

Mountain Road

In the mountains, no road
is straight. In the mountains

the line of gravel, of cracking
asphalt, follows when it can

the creek as the water turns
into the trees, out again

into those moments of sun, then
back, the shade so deep it is

like stepping into a darkened room.
In the mountains, one never sees

where one is going, even though
one always knows just how each turn

leads to the next and how to find
the scattered houses and whose

door will always open
if you knock and which doors

you may simply open, walk
in, sit down and be

there.

The Way Down

This time you are alone. The season
Over, the park in some legal sense closed.
The creek is just below the turn out
From the gravel road and you could
Walk down. The water would still be
Cold, but instead of the spring's opaque
Spray jumping the rocks to join the river,
The water now would be crystal, the granite
Knees and shoulders gleaming as if the gray
Were bright with color, and so you tie
The nylon shell to your waist, hang the nearly empty
Pack from your shoulders and start up the trail.
This late in the day there will be no one else
As you climb the switchbacks, the air cooling,
As your breath steadies into the day's motion
Like a tiny wheel within a pocket watch.

Where the trail dips a moment and the black
Berries leach the spring's spillage, you eddy
The hovering pool of gnats. Higher,
Above the fir trees, you cross a saddle,
The dirt so thin only the grass can breathe.
Then back into trees, the aspens,
Until you reach the small lake below the notch,

Where some winter storm has cut the slender
Trunks like hay scythed into tangled
Swaths waiting to be raked into stacks.

Walking on, you move again above
The trees, over a low ridge and up
To the smaller lake, the one where the two peaks
Rise as if from the water. You have chosen
The time carefully. The sun has finished
Its show, and the stilled water releases
The night. Your eyes can still see the strata
Of rock across the water and the drifts of scree,
The few small pines angling up from the steep face.
The retreating light touches the needles, a harpist
Brushing the strings. This is why
You've come—to hold out your arms,
The light on your wrists and hands
As if you too were of the music. For a moment,
You hear it. The cadenza. For a moment
You do not think of the way back down.

White Levis

The knees of her jeans are cut
to seem torn, the fadings processed
as if she's washed them over
and over. Caught between "Who,
Me?" and "Want some?" she is
trying to pose as she walks
past the park—a wavering
as the roller coaster slows, then
gathers for the sudden fall before the car
eases to a stop and the ride is over.

At thirteen I tossed newspapers
all summer, picked berries, apples, prunes,
then went to the one store in that town
that sold clothes. I bought lace up Field
& Stream boots, a rust plaid Pendleton
and white Levis, then walked past
the Pine Cone Café where the kids
already in high school played the jukebox
and drank cherry cokes. Perhaps
they saw me. Perhaps they already
knew that style is always ironic—

heat shimmers as the smoldering

trash catches fire, flaring the tiny sparks,
the cardboard wales of the box
glowing within the dark circle, then
darkening in on themselves.

Today I wear Levi 501s, button fly
shrink to fit. There´s stitching on the back
pockets. I wear a wide belt, a silver
buckle with an upside down T
in turquoise, as if it´s my initial,
my belt upside down and I´m too
stubborn to notice. If you asked,
I would tell you they're comfortable,
that the knees gave out only after weeks
of crawling to replace the floor.

I would not tell you it's because
my older cousin had a duck´s ass haircut,
sang rockabilly as if the California hills
were Tennessee, that his Model A
was a faded baby blue. I cannot help it
that Elvis has left the building and rockabilly
isn´t even retro anymore. I cannot help it that
the past didn´t stay present. I cannot help it
that my clothes overwrite my body and you
will read them however you damn well please

and get it wrong, because
I want you to.

And the buckle? It´s the upside
down "T" burned into the haunches
of the young cattle that will graze all summer
in the high mountains where the skin of snow
draws the spring grass and the two cowboys
keeping the herd will watch the sparks
from the twigs that boil the water in the tin
coffee pot.

Why Redneck Western Poets Write the Way We Do

for Betty Adcock

Because the preachers didn't come west
And our church is the baked shade
Under the firs behind the shed
Where the junked cars rust so slow
In the dry heat they are
Eternal and the low-growing thistle
Will never hide them.

Because everyone here knows
Who married who and who
Screwed who and every triumphant
Failure but nobody knows
Where they came from and everybody
Knows there is nowhere to go
But here.

Because the night sky is an abyss
Over the bar between here and nowhere
And when you sit in the cab of your truck
To clear your head enough to drive home
On a dark night the stars do not wink

Like fireflies but hang in the black crystal
No matter how much your head swims.

Because the day sky carries in heat
Shimmers across the ridges, and all
The markings of the ancient ice, of flood
And fire tell us we do not belong here,
But we have almost come to love the land
For refusing to take us in.

Because the sun melts the snow
From the rock above the tree line
And as the afternoon ebbs west
Down the face of the mountain
All we hear is silence.

CPSIA information can be obtained at www.ICGtesting.com
Printed in the USA
BVOW01s1220160414

350803BV00003B/431/P